# Human Highlight

# Human Highlight

an Ode to Dominique Wilkins

by

Idris Goodwin & Kevin Coval

Haymarket Books
Chicago, Illnois

Published in 2018 by
Haymarket Books
P.O. Box 180165
Chicago, IL 60618
www.haymarketbooks.org

ISBN: 978-1-60846-984-0

Trade distribution:
In the US, Consortium Book Sales and Distribution, www.cbsd.com
In Canada, Publishers Group Canada, www.pgcbooks.ca
In the UK, Turnaround Publisher Services, www.turnaround-uk.com
All other countries, Ingram Publisher Services International,
IPS_Intlsales@ingramcontent.com

This book was published with the generous support of Lannan
Foundation and Wallace Action Fund.

Cover art by Kamari Robertson.

10 9 8 7 6 5 4 3 2 1

# human highlight film

what is the electric that awakens us human?
all-of-a-sudden actors in a film
we didn't write. the sky, an aspiration, a light

high over the fields we work. our bodies human
in labor. to continue, we need a highlight,
a warm memory none can touch, a film

of the day. the way she bites her lip, a film
on loop, a lone highlight
we cradle to keep ourselves human,

sane. the dream to fly is human.
earth locked, we imagine what's high.
light from the sun, a guide, a residue. a film

we replay, endless sportscenter highlights.
a glimpse at the body free & more human,
a hope of our own boundlessness. the film

is receipt. King was human
Hank Aaron too. the city needs heroes, highlights
in a dark history. study the game film:

we are light, not deities on high. the film
a dark shield, a record. processor of sunlight. the reel:
we record everything. we are human, highlights.

# Of the Lord

Dominique mean "Of the Lord"
Latin rooted, French
Black like Haiti

We like our names with
Peaks, slopes, and vowels

We like our names to be ariel
And aural, throat and teeth and tongue
Our names gotta be songs

Serena Beyoncé Kobe Kareem Lebron
Abdul Kyrie Toussaint Andre
Kanye Rahasan

Names that melt résumés
Draymond DeAndre Desiree

Names that make Black conservatives
Turtle shell into shame
Shanice Latice Lashawna Latoya Kimani

Names that disrupt the roll call

Marshawn Aaliyah Malik Layla

Idris

Like names in holy books

Names that point to the world's faiths
Coalesced here on this stolen continent

The whole lexicon
The field, court, globe
Palmed but not dominated

Give us
Onomatopoeia names
Names with naps
Names that's laid
That give shade
Names that glide
Like Clyde
That fly like MJ sliding over the stars on Motown 25
Names with wings of predator birds
Names Like Dominique

# The First Slam Dunk Contest

Was held in Colorado

Olympians learn to breathe here
The altitude high like the air force
And the God fearing thousands

Here where air thin
Sky blue smeared white
and black noise
barely tolerated

So it's fitting
The dunk being what it is
Improvisation on a tightrope
so thin barely visible

The ground uneven here where
glares are not knives but worse
Where conversations veer on blacktops
Morph racial within minutes

Here where I improvise
contort, slide, make it in
by hell's height mere millimeters,
as I consider the velocity, power
consider the impact
And try to do it all with flair
With elegance
With poise
But enough grit to be memorable

Here where
My presence undeniable
neither grounded, in flight
always suspended midair
conscious of the spectators
Pondering every judge's verdict.

## the year of the snow jam
1982

all the white went away.

third pick, first round.
you didn't want to play
with the Jazz after college
in Georgia where the heat
& humidity stick like grits.

what funk would Utah offer.

you weighed offers like mothers
at the grocery with sweet peaches
on sweet Auburn, the richest
Blackest street in the world.
(no diggity.)

your move courted Black
hollywood south. it musta
been your long limb could
-give-a-fuck-less-ness.
your cool made you a hero,
an Outkast. your poster
a religious icon in the lair
of the Dungeon family
studio. your ability to defy
death & gravity woke
the imagination of a whole
people, city. four 50-win seasons
in a row. in a field, seeds
sowed. companies swooped

like Hawks. played the block
the city center, no Tree Rollins.
21 jerseys over khakis & rope
chains in the year crack became
a corporation.

you brought all the stars south.
love & hip-hop, a regional blues
a reality rap. opened studios
industries rebirthed a city, renewed
gentry-fried & high off the glint
& gloss of your Reebok pumps.

## the flattop

baby fresh bald
to topographic plateau.
lines cut like an equator.
tight curled crown. a bed
of soft springs or bent nails
wet coils. an air max brick
levitating séance. some
second scalp. extra inches
to guard the dome glistening.
terror in the sky mistaken
as a satellite rising to the rim
a second orange sun. the coif
of a deity ascending to the goal,
an ocean to stuff a rock thru.
the impossible made smooth
look like gravity gettin played.
made every barber chair
an alchemist's throne
a kind place to sit
& emerge a changed man.
the pyramid inverted
toppled. anything
was possible.

# The Kyle Garman

on Shermer rd, the only non-quick cut
not in a strip mall nor salon spot to get a straight razor
& bald fade was Tom & Rich's. Tom & Rich were both
old & white, at least seemingly old to me. both served
in the military, were proficient in shearing a man's head
with a blade, wore grey smocks & smelled like marlboro
men, thinning hair slicked over with pomade.

in the '91–'92 season
Kyle Garman was the coolest kid
in Glenbrook North. 3-letter varsity athlete,
quarterback & captain of the basketball team.
his senior year he scored impossible last second
buckets in back-to-back games to send us to super
-sectionals: the last 16 teams standing in the IL state.

Kyle would get a hightop bald fade in the first chair
at Tom & Rich's. his blond curls corkscrewed atop
his head like a golden crown so cold we just started
to ask for it: the Kyle Garman. a mess of floppy thin
-haired white boys trying to get it right. my own
dome wavy enough to muster a stand with a little bit
of gel. we were nowhere near as cool as Kyle

& leagues away from Dennis Rodman, David Robinson,
Kenny *Sky* Walker, Radio Raheem & even Jamar, the 7'1"
transfer student, one of 2 Black dudes on the team, lonely
in a sea of white boys. Jamar really wanted to play cello
to the chagrin of both his parents & our angry coaches.

we were all forced into some box, some small plateau
vision of the future; a life of middle management. i lived

across the street from Tom & Rich's, behind the White
Hen, in a row home. my front yard, a parking lot.
i'd stand outside for hours & practice dribbling a ball
or pen, wanting to get good enough at something
for long enough to leave.

## The '88 Tape

My great American novel
My brother and I rotate it steady
A choice cut from our growing stack

This tape, this duel, this concert
The black hawk and the bald bull
Trading riffs, cutting each other's head
Like United Center was Buddy Guy's Legends

We devour the rhythm, again and again
Sneakers, feet, clang of flesh, rubber and metal
The hands colliding in reverence
The stentorian AR 15 announcers
With their feigned control
Who speak of flared legs
Who speculate the judge's views

1988 was the final year
Dominique Wilkins and Michael Jordan
Having outscored Clyde The Glide Drexler and Otis Smith,
Spud Webb
In the finals, dueling, Dunk for dunk
As they had three years consistent.

Mike would win for the second year in a row
his reign looming ahead
Dominique returned two years later
Won his second title but not against the young franchise
Whose hands had begun to fill with champion rings

Dominique's shoes were never quite like Mike's
He never starred opposite Bugs Bunny or Mars Blackmon

Never led a team to George H. W.'s White House
But he had a molding hand
In the celestial who resurrected the game

# The Meaning of The Dunk

*Unbelievable creativity type of player*
—**Michael Jordan** on Dominique Wilkins

We didn't invent it but we evolved it
Like the woodwind
The turntable
The grind
The dance floor

The blacktop lab
For physics, bioscience
For thermodynamics
linguistic alchemy

The Dunk the flashback
To the playgrounds
Where bodies become heroic
Leaping across the canyon

They can't stop
 they can only hope to contain

The Dunk a fissure in time
A flashbulb
A call to celebrate
A juneteeth jubliee contained

elegance airlessness
The crowd holding its breath
In anticipation
before

The tympany
Boom

The outlawed boom
The percussion live in the balls of feet
The squeak of the sneaker prelude
Before lift off
And here come that boom
Televised
In real time
Can't take it back
Can't apologize
In your face

We taught this whole world to boom
To send reverbs / echoes through space

The dunk science fiction
The dunk disruption
Volcano in the ebb and flow
Of regularly scheduled function

It's the solo

Praise Bill Russell—Louis Armstrong
Wilt Chamberlain—Mingus
Dr. J—Dizzy
Dominique—Miles Davis

Notes floating free through space
Your eyes on the body
the slow mo canvas

Dark
In red

From the baseline

Michael Jordan—Coltrane
Spud Webb—Art Blakey
Rim shot
Darryl Dawkins—Cannonball
Shaquille O'Neal—George Clinton
the falling plexiglass
Showering over the heads
Baptizing the court
Christening the court
Under the jumbo screen watchful eye

Praise all the artist of air
The Dunk
freestyle cipher
Display of airlessness
Limitless
crafty br'er rabbit snatch, grab
A riddle
!Hallelujah!

Declaration
I am a man
Not a boy
I am alive
And defiant
A hero
I make deals with gravity
I rise and fall
The rim

The backboard
The game ain't over
But my name reverb
The Dunk is my signature

# Tomahawk

A tool to cut

Lord knows we live on them edges

That's what I see

Both arms, reaching back
Feet parallel, Torso ascending

Fueled by suspense
A warrior leap
Intent to decapitate

A body on the edge
Unable to turn back

Taking what's behind
The head, all that power

ego, resolve
To strike
any question
dead

# windmill

the ball plays peek-a-boo with the rim.
ripped under & over again. a rotational
force to conjure tornados. arms are blades
to generate electricity, extract jubilation
from fans mouths wide in wonder. an O
in the ocean, loopty-loop, roller coaster
waves crash in the air. Niq's feet firmly
planted in red paint, a step beneath
the dotted line. liftoff, Chicago Stadium,
a spring awakening, legs tucked, an Olympic
jump, the vicious swing of a heavy hammer
John Henry of the ballet. Niq an exclamation
point, a Black missile. the Spaulding; an asterisk,
a satellite in orbit. the body snaps at the hoop
a bear trap, matador lance, jaws of life hovering
above the court, a millennium falcon
an Atlanta Hawk.

# Alley Oop

Acrobats yelled it in the circus
Before defying death

But on the court
You can't preface

You gotta see it without looking
Ride the game's waves
And when summoned by your copilot
You gotta launch, hopeful but sure
You will join the conversation
Answer the call

Your job is acrobat
Catcher
Closer
Of a brief glorious arc

## 360°

madam i'm Adam
this eve in the garden Vince Carter
in Madison Square    pardon, i'm atlas in air
sky high on the shoulder, a boulder. my solos are perfect
8's. 180° one more again.
simpletons' posterized by Jason Richardson
WOW  mom
high flyin defiant Kobe Bryant, a top spot
new level, a tenet i'm in
the atmosphere: my gym,
like him or not, don't nod in the hop
/ scotch, pop shots, knock knock, who's there, rotator in air
borne dis-ease, make the world unease. it's Easy E.
check the stats, they're stacked, Nikki Minaj
that's a Drake bar, back to back, *oh man oh man*. under the
radar a mack,
make a meek mill at noon. back to bang at it.
gyration's a habit
dammit i'm mad. addict i whirl,
dervish to service this saga, impervious
Pervis not nervous Ralph Ellison's world.
invisible man. Able i'm seen. Cain's a maniac.
my cranium's magic. 1520 Sedgwick.
Herc's merry-go-round, the body in axis
double helix, a karmic principal made flesh
fresh: *what goes around comes back around again*.
tonight in the garden
madam, i'm Adam

# the year the dunk was outlawed
1967

*. . . to stop the six-foot-two brothers who
could dazzle the crowd & embarrass much
bigger white kids . . . they took it away.*
—Hunter College coach **Robert Bownes**

UCLA was 30–0
& Lew Alcindor had the wingspan
of a pterodactyl & the following summer
he'd boycott the olympics & take Shahada
to convert to Islam.

& the year before Bobby Seale & Huey Newton
met in a bakery & Texas Western beat Kentucky
& the specter of Black excellence dotted the tv
& america got a glimpse of what an equitable
playing field might begin to look like

& all the phog allen's & babe ruth's went
into the hysteria that builds prisons & creates
myopic mirages of shiny objects in hands
that hold air & continued policing Black
joy: no crossing the feet, no end zone
dancing, no fun bunch or Calinda chants
or Homer Jones spike. no Meadow Lark Lemon.

the ball was crystal, a peek
at reparations, a fear of a planet Black
& meritocratic. the ban prophetic
announcing an Afro-future: a yoke
on the admiral, a tomahawk on bird
every white center a prop

a posterized insult.
this kind of fly, a defiance
a flight risk. the league
cointelpro will try to ground
will grave, the gravity of the situation,
a temporary censor of the human
highlights yet to come

## Ode(s) to the extra muscle in Black people's legs that (allegedly) makes them better at sports

You remind us how susceptible
we be to the manufacture of myth

When inventive scholars exercise
inside phantom journals

Stir cauldron bottomless
melt down stereotypes
into chocolate fondue

pre information age
google was just a confident inflection

*Flex*

All them bricks
piled underneath
the driveway hoop
In our suburban
four bed house
is evidence
It ain't true

*Release*

I don't remember who first told me
But likely he was echoing a father
Or grandfather or uncle or some other kid

From our town of occasional Blacks

Likely while watching a jersey soar
Or marathon men of motherland
on the televised olympics

*Flex*

It couldn't be the
"twice as hard for half as much" theory
But rather an X-man mutation
Because how else

*Release*

Searching for your origin I find some believers
Who still maintain your existence
No.
Assure it
Because there was this one time
they saw this cloud of a Black man
Or because they came in 5th place
Or they were left dripping in the grey rain
Weakly gripping flaccid flowers

*Flex*

On Cotton and Football Fields
Kangaroo and Basketball court
flee or fight
either one, all of it,  performed in style

*Release*

Is there some kinda advantage?
Hell yeah
But it ain't rise on rested knees

# i want my father to retire

as you did in Greece. paunch beneath
your jersey. sweatier than the youth
you regal in the locker room with stories
about Spud & the night you made Bird
obsolete. after a shower & ice rub down,
a post-game meal at Strofi overlooking
the Acropolis, swirling Ouzo in a snifter
dotted with espresso beans, a white
linen tablecloth dotted with candles
surrounded by Senegalese immigrants
who hustle wood sculpted religious
depictions of the mother out Black
garbage bags for white tourists.
your shoes butter leather smooth.
molded like clay to your tired feet.
the oil on the table's infused with lemon
peels & rosemary. not too much salt
on the Souvlaki. your blood pressure
manageable. candles shoot shadows
into the valley, off your face lit
with laughter. maybe an autograph or two
but mostly the tingle of Mavrodafni, a plate
of feta and bougatsa. mostly a long night
beneath the stars & the company
of women who speak multiple tongues.

# tbh

*an assist*

1.

i'm not saying it was a conspiracy
some home cooking, sending Air to orbit
a brand, rocket launched. it's facts his grace
cockpit from the foul line more iconic
than neil armstrong's walk, i mean
Mike flew. his sneaks dangling above
our head like the price tag we were smart
enough not to even ask moms about.

but check the technique, Dominique
a thunder clap, rim rattler vanguard
band leader Dancer, Dixon, Rudolph
the screws off, the backboard, Black
soars, sinew wave crash on the hard
court below.

kept us high, electric wide. we stepped inside
the mess, bent to glide. Clyde Frazier
juice on loan for a generation like the rest
was rent to buy. judges buggin pssssssst
pests aside, you threw up a W
like the western side. the best of guys,
hopped the train in Chi, looked inside the closing
doors & took the L in stride. Mike the GOAT
& like you slashin to the rim, these facts
you can't deny.

i got all sorts of hometown midwest pride,
but to see you fly, mystique on fleek

a miracle like the Cubs won. but Dominique
let's keep it a Buck, like Sidney Moncrief.
the dunk contest is dumb fun, but tbh,
'88 all-star game weekend, G, you won.

2.

One hand clutching One sphere
and no fear, transcending years

You won, scores is just numbers
the performance timeless

I show my son them 88 clips
and when that inner light flips
time slips to future

past and present / I can't play—at all
been shooting 30 years / still the ball veers
and still there's / this voice that spills
possibility / one / day I will be Bird accurate

every time the sneakers squeeze
these flat feet / and my son follows me
to the driveway / where we attempt / leap and pass
time / passes / rhymes / of our heroes

We ain't trying to be
we are makin highlights between us
when I lift him to the hoop to dunk
I am him and he is me
we are one

**IDRIS GOODWIN** was voted most improved player at Isiah Thomas basketball camp in the summer of 1988. Since then he's become an award-winning playwright, breakbeat poet, and essayist. He is the author of the Pushcart-nominated essay collection *These Are The Breaks* (Write Bloody Books), and the echapbook *Inauguration* cowritten with Nico Wilkinson (Haymarket Books), which won a literary award from Pikes Peak Arts Council. He's appeared on HBO, the Discovery Channel, and Sesame Street. His widely produced stageplays include: *How We Got On, This is Modern Art* (cowritten with Kevin Coval), *Blackademics*, and *Bars and Measures*. His play *And In This Corner Cassius Clay* received the 2017 Distinguished New Play Award from the American Association of Theater and Education. Idris is a regular contributor to NPR affiliate KRCC in Colorado Springs and assistant professor in the Department of Theater and Dance at Colorado College. Find him on social media or at idrisgoodwin.com.

**KEVIN COVAL** played semi-pro ball in Wales in the mid-90s which says more about the condition of ball in Wales at the time then it does about his game. Coval is also the author of ten books including *A People's History of Chicago*, editor of *The BreakBeat Poets: New American Poetry in the Age of Hip-Hop*, & cowrote the play, *This is Modern Art* with Idris Goodwin. Coval is the Artistic Director of Young Chicago Authors, winner of a MacArthur Award for Creative & Effective Institutions, and the founder of Louder Than A Bomb: The Chicago Youth Poetry Festival. He cohosts the podcast *The Cornerstore* on WGN Radio. His work has appeared on *The Daily Show*, four seasons of HBO's *Def Poetry Jam*, CNN.com, *Poetry Magazine* & *Fake Shore Drive*. He teaches hip-hop poetics in high schools, colleges, & community centers around the globe. Find him on the interconnected networks @kevincoval.

CPSIA information can be obtained
at www.ICGtesting.com
Printed in the USA
LVOW13s0328010218
564502LV00008B/135/P